the ME problen

by Rob Warner

CONTENTS

Cover design: Ross Advertising and Design Limited ·
Designer: Paul Edwards · Inside illustrations: Paulo Baigent ·
Typeset by HWTypesetters, Norwich · Printed by Ebenezer Baylis & Son
Limited, The Trinity Press, Worcester and London ·
 · ISBN 086201 820 X

the me problem

I N T R O

If you met someone with no problems in life, no struggles as a Christian, there's one thing you could be sure about: they'd be no good writing about the 'me problem'. As for me, on a bad day my children tell me I'm the biggest problem they've got!

Today's world is getting desperate. The only thing that seems to be falling apart faster than the planet is human relationships. If we did sort out the ecological crisis, would the human race still know not just how to fall in love, but how to *stay* in love? As designer drugs hit the streets in ever larger quantities and growing numbers of young teenagers are trying them out, will anyone risk having children any more? As cities in the States and Britain are rocked by corruption in business and the courts, with race-hatred on the streets, and a growing under-class of the desperately poor, will anyone want to live in cities any more? It's not difficult to feel, even after the end of the cold war, that the days might be numbered for civilization on planet Earth.

But what have these global crises got to do with *me*? There doesn't seem anything much I can do about them, so should I simply avoid the newspapers, or read them and get gloomy? Many people avoid the 'me' problem by blaming someone else, or by hoping for things to get better soon once there's the right economic system or government. However, the collapse of communism and the failures of capitalism, the injustices which tarnish every society, reflect a more pessimistic truth: the biggest problem we face is not how to improve a political or economic system, but how to deal with the selfishness in the human heart. Some years ago *The Times* ran a series of letters on the theme 'What's wrong with the world?' The shortest was from G K Chesterton, the Christian author, who wrote: 'Sir, I am'.

As Christians we believe that Jesus Christ – the great 'I am' – is the hope of the world. In him alone is the solution to our deepest needs. For the problem of the human condition is found not simply in evil dictators or corrupt systems, but in ordinary people like each one of us. Thank God that the sin problem has a sin answer, in Jesus Christ being made sin for our sake on the cross.

SIN PROBLEM

As a young believer, I reached the brink of giving up. I found it hard to be a disciple of Jesus, and yet it seemed easy for others in my youth group. The conclusion I came to was that Christian living must come naturally to them. After all, no one was even hinting at any difficulties with sin and temptation. But it certainly wasn't easy or natural for me.

For about six months I dropped out of church. There seemed no point going on with the struggle, since obviously I must simply be different from other Christians. What was happening was that I'd made an unwelcome discovery, one of the most important discoveries you can make as a Christian. The biggest problem in life, the biggest hurdle to living for Jesus, was (*and continues to be*) *ME!*

The 'me' problem that made me feel like giving up on Christianity, later brought me to recommitment. The reason was simple: left to my own devices I was stuck with my own selfish nature, with no real hope of change. So I came back to Christ and yielded my life afresh to his Lordship, realising more than ever before that I needed God's forgiveness. Knowing also that the only way I can come to Christ, today and every day, is just as I am, relying on him to accept me and to sort me out.

Should you come to the point when

you know deep down what this 'me' problem is all about, take courage. Many others have been there before, and it's a necessary part of self-discovery in Christ.

SELF-IMAGE PROBLEM

Forgiveness is only half the story. Bestseller lists today are top heavy with books about how to improve your self-image. Some dismiss this as self-indulgence, just another example of sin and pride. But I think there's more to it than that.

We live in a world where growing numbers of marriages and friendships are marked by three unnerving qualities: they are fragile, short-lived and disappointing. But it's in relationships that we actually discover and know ourselves. So when more and more adults come from homes that are broken or breaking, and when the average stay in any house is about five years, the network of secure relationships that we need as a solid foundation for self-acceptance is eroded and destroyed.

Look around any crowded train, or any checkout queue, and behind the blank faces you're looking at hurting people. Some may have bookshelves crammed with guides on gaining self-worth; others could be handing over their money in the counselling boom mushrooming across the Western world today; still more frantically seek assurance of their self-worth through casual sex or an affair with someone younger. It's not simply that they just need someone to love. In their heart of hearts, men and women need to know that someone could, and does, really love *them.*

The Christian gospel has wonderful answers to this ache in the human heart. We can explain that no one was ever conceived as an accident, or as the product of a genetic game of chance. On the contrary, each person is special, knitted together in a mother's womb by a God of love (Psalm 139:13). We can discover the astonishing extent of God's love for each individual: that God loves *us* as much as he loves Jesus (John 17:23). And we can encounter the demonstration of that love, first of all on the pages of human history, when Christ died for us even though we had rebelled against Father God, but also in the here and now, as God pours his love into our hearts by the Holy Spirit (Romans 5:5).

ME POTENTIAL

My prayer is that these daily readings will help you to grow in self-understanding, grow in knowledge of God's mercy and forgiveness, and grow in confidence in your potential as a new creation in Christ. The readings are based on my favourite translation of the Bible, the New International Version, but you can just as well use another version if you prefer.

One thing you don't have to do is to use this booklet on your own. If possible, seek out a mature Christian in your church who can support you. It would be great if you could meet to share and pray once a week, maybe for just half-an-hour. That way you'll receive personal support as you make this vital journey of discovery, in which the *me problem* of your sinful nature will turn into the *me potential*, as you explore how to become a winner in the service of Christ.

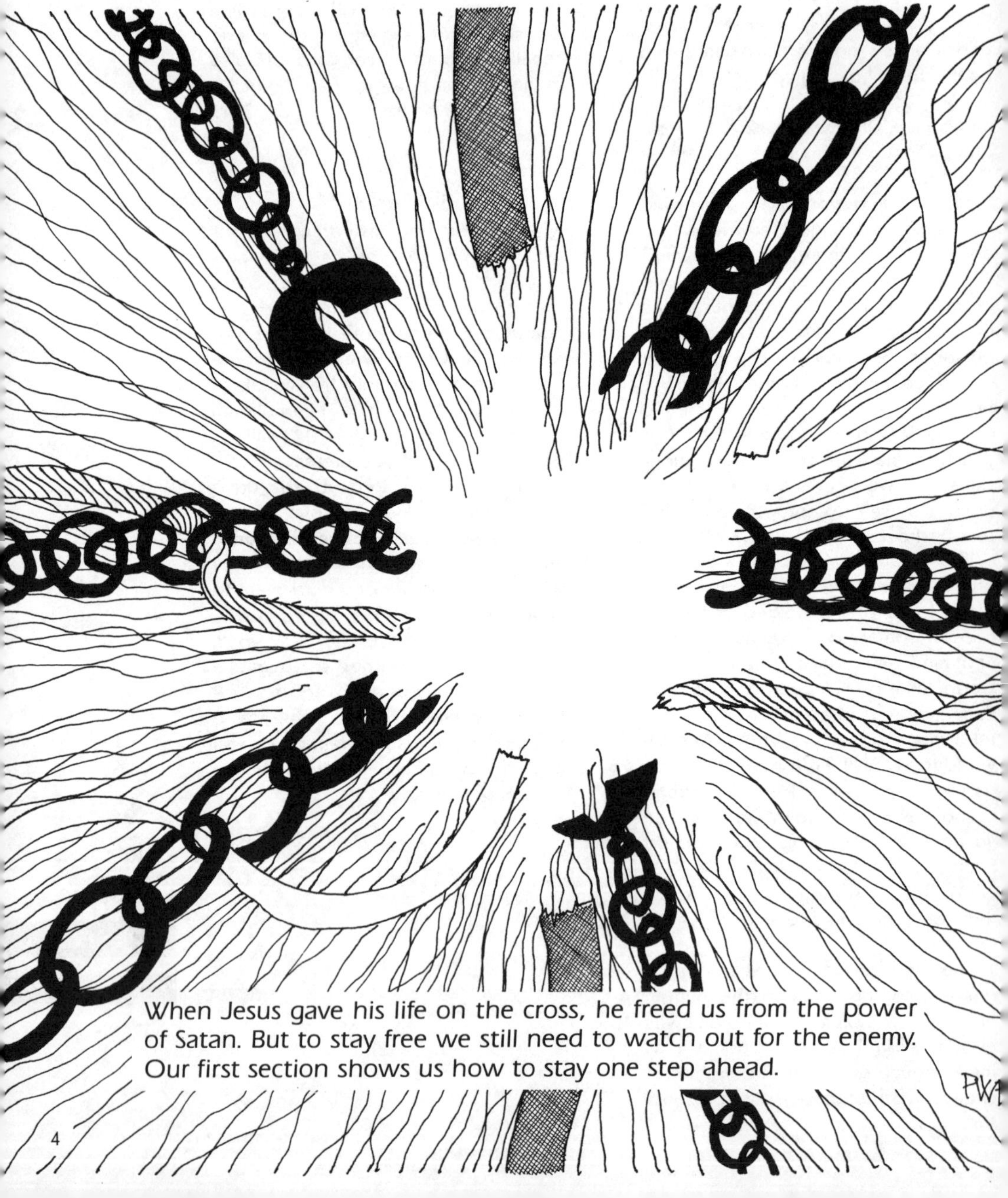

When Jesus gave his life on the cross, he freed us from the power of Satan. But to stay free we still need to watch out for the enemy. Our first section shows us how to stay one step ahead.

ou can be free!

When Sam was converted, you couldn't miss the change in his life. He was confident that every sin had been forgiven, and he found in Christ a joy he'd never known before.

Sam was right when he said he'd been given a fresh start. But sadly, there was a problem.

Much less helpful was his confidence that sin in his life was now history. When he did slip back into old ways, he wondered whether he'd ever been a Christian at all.

Susan's crisis was a particular sin. She'd been flattered by the attention her new boss gave her, and one thing led to another. She'd drifted into the affair without ever thinking through the consequences, but now she couldn't think about anything else. She'd changed job and the relationship was over, but she felt branded with shame. On Sundays she often had to fight back the tears but didn't dare explain to anyone. If they knew, she feared the church would throw her out in disgust.

If we are to know what it means to be free, there are two things we need to be quite clear about as Christians: the power of sin *and* the power of forgiveness.

POWER OF SIN

Without a clear sense of the power of sin, we'll face needless disappointment as a follower of Jesus. The apostle Paul describes the kind of inner turmoil we might face (Romans 7:7-25). He explains that inside us is a sinful nature, and when it hears the law of God it reacts by longing to do those very things that are forbidden.

Some people suggest Paul is talking about life before conversion. But, if I look into my own life, I know for sure that the sinful nature still lurks within. We know the Christian life is a fight *outwardly.* We are constantly faced with the pressure to fit in with what everyone else is doing. We know, too, that Satan is ever ready to throw temptation in our way. But it is vitally important to understand that we're also fighting on the *inside*.

From the moment we are born again in Jesus, we possess a double nature. Deep in our inner being we've been made new by Christ, so that we can love God and delight in living Jesus' way (Romans 7:22). But we also find evil within, dragging us away from Father God (Romans 7:19, 21). In fact, this sinful nature is so desperately hostile to our new life that Paul says it's as though there was a civil war going on inside us (Romans 7:23).

But this sinful nature is no longer in charge. Like a wild beast that's cornered, it puts up a vigorous struggle, yet its strength is limited, its days are numbered by the victory of Christ's death and resurrection. This civil war is definitely not being fought between rival forces of *equal* power. However, even though the scales are

the me problem

firmly tipped to the ultimate triumph of good, the war inside every believer is still very real.

One great Christian leader, Augustine, discovered that the longer he was a Christian and the closer he walked with God, the more acutely aware he became of the struggle within. And so he prayed the following, not simply on the day of his conversion, but as a mature believer: 'Help me... I have now become a problem to myself.'

Once we recognise we have a sinful nature, we can start to fight it. Fight with prayer, fight by choosing the good, and by avoiding those situations which regularly tempt us.

POWER OF FORGIVENESS

It should be reassuring to every Christian to read the following warning in the New Testament.

'If we claim to be without sin, we deceive ourselves and the truth is not in us' (1 John 1:8).

But that's not all. As John goes on to explain, '... if anybody does sin, we have one who speaks to the Father in our defence - Jesus Christ, the Righteous One. He is the atoning sacrifice for our sins...' (1 John 2:1, 2).

When we become Christians, it's no good coming to God parading good works. Rather, we must be ready to confess our sin and declare our trust in Christ, who died in our place, taking our punishment. Our confidence should not be in our own merits, but in the righteousness of Jesus Christ.

What's true in conversion is true in Christian living. It would be absurd to imagine, that having started out by trusting in Christ's sacrifice for us, later on we should put our confidence in ourselves. But in practice that happens. I often meet believers who have fallen into the trap of trusting in their own goodness: who *they* are, or what *they* have done for God. Some swell with religious pride, others sink into despair when this misplaced confidence collapses.

Please don't fall into such traps! We can be confident that we are loved by a merciful God - in spite of the sinful nature struggling within us - simply and only because of the power of the death of Jesus Christ. Any other grounds for confidence will cause us to slip and slide. The only answer is to put all our trust in the crucified and risen Saviour, that way our confidence is in the unshakable one.

Whether you've done something particular of which you are ashamed, or whether you are struggling with a general sense of sin, remember, Jesus really can forgive and restore you. Because Christ is our sin-bearer, he has the power to cancel absolutely *every* single trace of sin. So keep fighting the sinful nature, and keep trusting in your totally reliable Saviour!

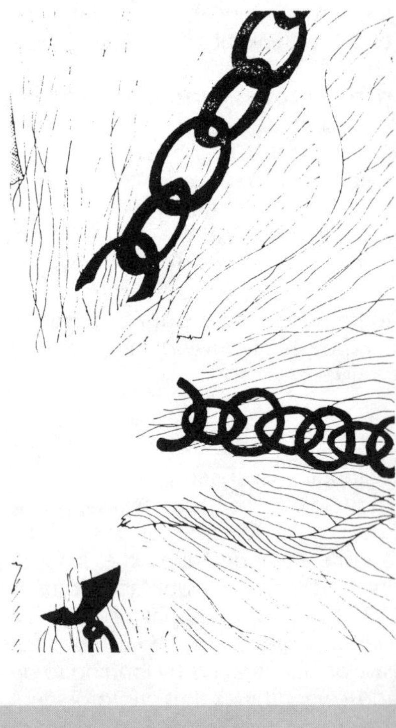

Day 1
THE TRUTH SETS US FREE
John 8:31-47

As communism collapsed in Eastern Europe, the cry for freedom rang out loud and clear. Other nations took up the shout, and many dictators have trembled. But Jesus presents a stark truth: our ultimate captivity is neither political nor economic. The greatest problem is deeper and universal: we are slaves of sin.

This claim is not the quickest way to win friends and influence people. In fact, the crowd was so incensed they were ready to kill Jesus. The God of Abraham, they protested, was simply bound to respect their pedigree: 'Abraham is our father.' Just as a British passport speeds us through Heathrow airport, they thought that being a Jew was enough to win God's favour.

In the same way, some still think that being English, coming from a 'respectable' home, or going to church is enough to guarantee God's favour. Yet...

False hopes set no one free. You can't begin to discover Jesus' freedom until you accept this unpalatable truth: the biggest problem in your life is you. However, it's not insurmountable – with Jesus you can be the kind of person God wants you to be. But you have to work at it and allow the Holy Spirit to take control.

Prayer starter:

Thank you, Jesus, that you help us face the *me problem*, not to grind us underfoot but to set us free.

Day 2
STAY TUNED
James 4:1-10

As a teenager I had a beaten-up old radio that wouldn't stay tuned, held together with sticky tape. I used to listen with one hand on the dial, tracking the signal through the crackle and hum.

In the same way, we need to concentrate on staying tuned as believers. You know what it's like: we begin to drift, distracted by the cares or fun of life. That's why James spells out the need to practise the presence of God. Reception will deteriorate if you neglect this discipline: keep close to him.

We stay tuned as we:

- come to our heavenly Father in prayer daily
- meet with other Christians to praise and worship God
- listen to those who teach us more about our faith
- deal with the sins in our life that hold us back from following Jesus
- obey God, trusting that he knows what is best for us

Even so, staying tuned is only half the story. We have joined God's army and there's a war on. Battle wages on three fronts. Internally, our sinful nature fires up destructive desires (vs 1-3); the values of society seek to entrap us (vs 4, 5), and evil spiritual forces are on the attack. But we are protected by the victory and authority of Jesus, so keep resisting!

Prayer starter:

Use verses 8 to 10 as a basis for your prayer time with God.

the
me
problem

Day 3
FACE THE TEST
Luke 22:31-34

If there's one thing that can be guaranteed in life, it's mistakes. In the Christian life, that means we are going to let God down. We don't lose our sinful nature at conversion. Rather, we begin a lifelong struggle with it.

When you let God down badly, you can feel devastated, convinced you are not useful to Christ any more. But the secret of holiness is this: however many times you fail, you *can* return to Jesus – he is always ready to forgive and take us back into active service.

Peter's threefold denial comes as a necessary warning to every believer. Our Christian walk will be marred by sin. But Jesus promised that if we repent, there's still work for us to do (John 21:15-17).

Meditation:

The other side of failure is a fresh start for those who belong to Christ. 'And when you have turned back, strengthen your brothers' (Luke 22:32).

Jot down anything that comes to mind which you know you need to 'turn back' from. Spend some time meditating on Hebrews 12:1-6 for encouragement in your struggle against sin.

Now move in your thoughts from yourself to your brothers and sisters in Christ: are there any in your fellowship who particularly need your support? In what ways could you be a 'strengthener' to them? Remember, your commitment to help may need to be long-term rather than a one-off burst.

Day 4
STAND FIRM
1 Peter 5:8-11

'Freedom to do whatever I want' comes high on most people's priorities. But the Bible redefines freedom. Live for ourselves and we end up slaves of sin. Surrender our lives to God, and we discover perfect freedom in Christ's service.

Though headstrong when young, Peter had learned the lesson of true freedom. And so he invites us to be self-controlled rather than self-indulgent, for to be truly free means humbly submitting ourselves to Christ.

Satan hates the freedom of God's children, and like a roaring lion, he longs to get his teeth into us. The terrible beauty of a lion's roar strikes fear into the vulnerable. Such fear unnerved Peter on the night of Jesus' trial, when three times he denied knowing Jesus.

Satan loves to stir up fear. Think of times he has done this in your life. Now, remember, the lion is chained. Let him roar all he likes, for if you stay alert and keep your distance, he cannot destroy you. Stand firm in the victory of your risen Lord, and those fears and temptations will lose their grip and power over you.

Prayer starter:

We rest in you, our shield and our defender
We do not go, alone against the foe.
Strong in your strength, safe in your keeping tender,
We rest in you, and in your name we go.

E Cherry (1872–97)

Day 5

HOLD ON TO GOD'S PROMISE

1 Corinthians 10:1-13

'I knew it was wrong, but I couldn't help myself!'

Few people like to face up to their own responsibility for sin. We flatter ourselves that the tide of temptation is too great for us to resist. But Paul explains that our temptations are just like everyone else's, because the tempter repeats the same old tricks.

God sets limits on the devil. He knows what we can cope with but leaves us with a vital decision: will temptation be the gateway to sin, or the door to freedom?

Escape lanes on steep hills protect lorries hurtling towards disaster. In the same way, God provides ways of escape so that life needn't slide out of control when temptation strikes.

The word which is translated as 'temptation' also means 'testing'. When a train first enters a long, curved tunnel, the driver can't see light ahead. If you can't see an end to your time of testing, don't despair. Hold fast to the promise of God, and soon you will see light at the end of the tunnel.

Prayer starter:

Thank you, Lord Jesus, that when temptation is strongest, you are stronger still.

Continue in prayer as you reflect on verse 13. Think about God's faithfulness, the times he has stood by you as you have placed your trust in him. Thank him for his help in the past and take hold of his strength for the present.

Day 6

THE DEATH OF DEATH

Hebrews 2:14-18

Many people today are held in a terrible bondage by the fear of death.

Frank's dad collapsed and died at 42. When Frank's own 42nd birthday was near he couldn't sleep – overcome by the fear that he, too, would die young.

Martha's mum was well past eighty and getting frail, but Martha became very defensive if anyone hinted that her mum might not live for ever.

When Jesus was in his early thirties, the political and religious authorities plotted his execution. The crowds turned against him. His followers fled in disarray. The demonic hosts must have been jubilant; where temptation had failed, surely death would crush the Son of God. The cross is a sign of contradiction, the ultimate victory snatched from the jaws of apparent defeat. Because Jesus' death on the cross led to his resurrection, death is no longer the end but the beginning; no longer the denial of life but the gateway to the abundant life of heaven.

Because Jesus' death also pays the price of sin, he sets us free not only from the fear of death but also from the fear of condemnation. If we put our trust in the crucified Son of God, we really are free indeed! And this freedom to live as God's child should bring peace and joy that is evident to those we meet.

Prayer starter:

Lord Jesus, conqueror of death, release me from my fears... that in my daily living I might know and show the freedom you have won for me.

extra

Confession tactics

Guilt for unconfessed sin is like wearing a heavy rucksack. The longer it's there, the more it weighs you down.

HAND IT OVER! Some Christians are carrying an unnecessary burden. Because they feel ashamed of their sin, they keep it tucked away out of sight. But the weight of secret guilt takes away the joy of salvation. It can even take away our confidence that we ever became a Christian.

So, when it comes to confessing sin, it's definitely a case of the sooner the better. It's only when we hand over our sin that Jesus can deal with it and we can receive his forgiveness.

THE RIGHT APPROACH Here are some approaches to confession that I find useful:

- *Use* the last two verses of Psalm 139 as a personal prayer and then be still before God.
- *Write* a letter to God declaring your sin. Then, as you pray in repentance and seek Christ's forgiveness, tear it up or, even better, set fire to it as a sign that confessed sin is taken away from you forever.
- *Get together.* If you're finding it difficult to believe that your responsibility for a particular sin can be taken away, ask a leader from your church to talk and pray with you.

Day 7

WINNING TEAM

Ephesians 6:10-20

In American football there's a golden rule: no matter how large the player bearing down on you, you have to stand your ground! As members of Christ's army, our responsibility too is to stand firm whatever Satan hurls at us.

Even the most hardened American football player wouldn't dream of entering a game without putting on his elaborate kit. No armour, no hope! It's just the same in spiritual warfare.

Roman shields had a ridged edge. They could be locked together as a wall before an advancing army, or linked overhead to protect against a flight of arrows. Sometimes Christians waste energy fighting each other and miss out, for our armour is most effective when we take our stand *together.* If we link our shields of faith, we have the resources in Christ to repel *every* assault of Satan.

An attacking Roman soldier also needed a good sword. Paul had this in mind when he described the Bible as the Christian's 'good' sword – the sword of the Spirit. To be an effective Christian we need to 'take hold' of God's truths and promises and use them in moments of opportunity and need.

Prayer starter:

Lord Jesus, I will take my stand in your resurrection victory. Help me to grow strong by the Word and the Spirit.

Who's in charge?

If we are honest, all of us are too concerned with 'number one'. But dealing with the 'me' problem means things have to change. How to work at making Christ Lord in every area of life is the theme for section two.

W

the me problem

When Sinatra sang 'My Way' he did more than discover the perfect song with which to bring to a climax his retirement concerts for many years to come. He gave an anthem for the late twentieth century: the age of the triumph of individualism.

Ours is a society where birth is no longer destiny, for society tells us that we, as today's people, are free to make our own choices, free to shape our own lives and to choose our own careers. We are free to marry who we like, marry more than once, or live together without marrying at all. We are free to preserve or destroy the foetus sheltering in its mother's womb. Old fashioned restrictions have been torn away in the name of the freedom of the individual.

PRICE TO PAY

When everyone demands the right to run their own life, their own way, this freedom exacts a high price. Some have denied the reality of the 'responsible society', calling for everyone to look out for themselves.

The tyranny of individualism is tearing the heart out of relationships. It's hardly surprising that so many marriages are under severe strain, for today's values leave little room for putting your partner before yourself.

What's more, in an age of rights before responsibilities, some children are drowning in toys but starved of affection. Yet these are the lucky ones. In the part of London where I work, for every live birth another baby has been killed in the womb. In spite of all the assurances to the contrary, abortion today has become for many just another means of contraception.

At the same time, the experience of community is becoming a dim memory, at least in our cities. As individuals lead increasingly separate and isolated lives, it's getting harder even to discover your neighbours' names. The triumph of individualism has littered the world with lonely people.

IT'S UP TO ME!

Today's values go deeper. It's not just that we all want to make our own choices. Our society has come to believe that there aren't any absolute moral values. Instead, people claim the right to choose their own values. In fact, the one unforgivable sin is to presume to impose your values on anyone else. The cry of our age is that if it works for you, that's great, but you must make sure, like Sinatra, that you do it your way and leave others to do it *their* way.

This is very far from any Christian understanding of how to live life to the full. Because there is a creator God high over all, he has every right to set standards for his subjects. Those standards are revealed in the Bible, not as a random set of rules and restrictions, but as God's guidelines to make the most of life.

What's more, submitting to Jesus as Lord does more than set a new direction for our individual lives. God's purpose is not simply that we sing: 'I did it Christ's way.' Rather, we are saved personally in order to enter into a whole set of new relationships, as members of the body of Christ. That means, it's only *together* that we can fully 'do it Christ's way'.

io's in charge?

VALUES IN QUESTION

There are two megaphones for today's values. The first is *advertising,* where what matters most in society is made crystal clear. The second is *children,* since children sometimes let slip the unvarnished values their parents have shaped for them, stripped of the discreet camouflage of the adult world. And that can be very disconcerting!

So what values are under threat from Jesus as Lord? Maybe you will recognise one of the following:

- Many are driven by money and success, so that these priorities shape their lives and determine their most important decisions.
- Some establish their own self-worth through competing with everyone around them, finding their own place in life's pecking-order, and looking down on everyone beneath them.
- Some go in for power-parenting, living out their own unfulfilled ambitions through their children, pressuring them into ever more clubs or examinations, and never letting an opportunity pass to tell other parents of their children's remarkable accomplishments.
- Some see life through deep-rooted racial prejudice, while others cannot speak to a woman without patronising her.
- Some store up a lifetime's resentment in their hearts, forever taking new offence and nursing grudges, old and new.
- Some are trapped by petty legalism which sometimes contaminates churches, bringing with it a negative and critical spirit, always thinking the worst and speaking judgment on others.

Such things are intruders that deserve no room in our new life in Christ. I'm so glad that Jesus has the authority to evict them, each and every one!

LIVING LORD

If we are serious about serving Jesus as Lord, we begin to discover some glorious truths:

- We live in a world of moral confusion and much personal hurt. But, when Jesus is Lord, we discover a new safety.
- We live in a world that cries freedom but knows only bondage to sin. But, as believers, we begin to discover that Jesus spells freedom, for it's only in his service that we are truly free.
- What's more, in a world which knows no ultimate satisfaction, we can discover true fulfilment. Jesus promised to all who choose to follow him as Lord: 'I have come that they may have life, and have it to the full' (John 10:10).

I invite you to examine your life and values this coming week, to see if any changes need to be made, in order to live for Jesus, with him as your only Lord and Master.

Day 8

MAKE CHRIST LORD

Luke 6:46-49

[redacted]

the me problem

I heard this honest assessment from a company director. 'At home it's Christ first, my wife second and my business third. In the office it's the reverse.'

Many employers today demand absolute loyalty. If they offer promotion, the only response expected is 'Thank you'. If they ask you to move to the other end of the country, they only expect one question. 'When?'

Scratch the surface of a nominal Christian's life and you'll find the world's values under religious varnish. Some are slaves to ambition, some to fashion, and some to the latest home improvement. Some simply must have whatever advertisers are pushing.

We really don't have to let the world call our tune. If Jesus is our Lord, we are living under a higher authority. Consult him first before you say 'yes' to the demands of advertising or to the pressures of work.

It's not that Christ is opposed to every successful career. But that should not be our highest priority. Whatever we do each day, we need to see ourselves as a missionary, sent as a servant of Christ to be salt and light, and to be the bringer of good news to those around us (Matthew 5:13-16).

Prayer starter:

Rescue me, Lord Jesus. Help me understand that where my values are not your values then my life is built on sand.

Day 9

LORD OF CREATION

Colossians 1:15-17

Long before he came to earth, the Son of God was at work. If the breadth of the work of Christ surprises you, then it can only mean *one* thing: your Christ is too small! Spend some time thinking about:

- Christ – the *agent* of creation.

Through him all things have been made. From air to angels, everything ultimately owes its existence to Christ.

- Christ – the *head* of creation.

He's the boss, and humans are ultimately under his authority, even though we have rebelled against him. What's more, all created things, from the nucleus of each atom to the most distant planet, are designed to resound with a song of praise to Christ.

- Christ – the *sustainer* of creation.

Creation isn't like a clock that God wound up and then left to its own devices. Christ *stays* involved. Our life and the continued existence of the entire cosmos are a fresh gift from God each day.

Thought for the day:

Christians should be more concerned about the environment than anyone else, for Christ is Lord of creation.

What does this mean in practical terms? Make a note of three things you could be doing. Pray about them and, perhaps, talk them over with some Christian friends in your church.

Day 10
LORD OF THE CHURCH
Colossians 1:18-23

The Lord of creation is also Lord of the new creation.

- Christ – the *agent* of the church.

His death and resurrection make our salvation possible. Only Jesus can do this.

- Christ – the *head* of the church.

He's in charge of those he has redeemed. He claims the right to be the Lord of your life and Lord in your local church. Whatever method of decision-making your church has, it's important to keep in view the absolute Lordship of Christ. As the church submits to Christ, our purpose is to bring glory to the one who won salvation for us.

- Christ – the *sustainer* of the church.

When you feel weak, Christ wants to be your strength and inspiration. He keeps his people going, sending the Spirit upon us with every encouragement. When you feel weak, Christ wants to be both your inspiration and your inspirer, to build your character and your gifts.

Prayer starter:
Lord Jesus Christ, your power is so vast and your work is so great, yet still you care for me.

Help me today to trust in your death, to submit to your Lordship, and to be filled with your Spirit, so that I may live to the praise of your glory.

Day 11
LORD OF MY LIFE
Colossians 2:6-19

Throughout life we take on board a set of values we assume are 'normal'. These instinctive values are further developed and reinforced through our upbringing and schooling, through advertising and the media. But such values can become deeply opposed to the way of Christ (v 8). Consider these values:

- *Materialism* – where quality of life is measured in material things. It's what you've got that measures not only your happiness but also your worth as a person.
- *Consumerism* – when a self-centred society always asks the same question: 'What's in it for me?' Personal relationships are often redefined not as loving commitments but as short-term opportunities for self-gain. Consumer Christians have the same attitude to their local church.
- *Individualism* – when we claim: 'No one is going to interfere with my life! I'll do whatever I like!'

Where Christ is truly Lord we become an alternative society, but if the world's values take us captive, our spiritual sap will shrink and our thankfulness will wither. It makes sense to root ourselves in Christ as Lord of daily life.

Thought for the day:
As a disciple of Christ, which wrong values in your favourite TV programme do you need to resist?

the
me
problem

Day 12

NEGATIVE RELIGION

Colossians 2:20-3:4

Religion easily degenerates into a list of rules. And those rules are all about what is forbidden. True, God has revealed in the Bible certain limits to human behaviour which we ignore at our peril. But, when Christian faith turns into a religion of negatives, it becomes sour.

It's not just the burden of legalism, or the avoidance of all the good pleasures which Jesus himself enjoyed, like laughter, wine and good food with friends. What's worst is the crushing burden of a negative spirit, which finds fault with everything and knows no joy in Christ. Paul's reaction to negative religion is outspoken: it doesn't work, and has nothing to do with Christ.

What's more, the Christian has a liberating choice to make (vs 1, 2). We can break free from the life-crushing negatives of man-made religion and discover Jesus-style holiness.

Minor problems and petty arguments should not be allowed to spoil our witness or control our thoughts. We should resolve to live our new life, focused on all that Christ has won for us.

Prayer starter:

Lord Jesus, help me to break free from a religion of negatives, to bask in the glory of your mercy and love, and to know the abundance of life which you have promised.

Day 13

SERVE HIM AS LORD - 1

Matthew 4:18-22

Following Jesus is basic to discipleship. We can't live a productive Christian life if we are trying to do things for Jesus without first making sure we are walking close to him day by day.

When Jesus invited the fishermen to follow him, they didn't need asking twice. Peter later summed up the joyful sacrifice of serving Jesus as Lord: 'We have left everything to follow you!' (Matthew 19:27)

For us, it may not be 'everything', but there is sure to be 'something'. We need to keep in step with Jesus and stay close to him in whatever we are doing.

What Jesus offered the first disciples was not only a new relationship, but a new priority as 'fishers of men'. This means that following Jesus includes the specific task of world evangelisation – we can begin with our friends! We won't be good followers without staying intimate with Jesus; and we can't be really close to Jesus if we are indifferent to the needs of the lost.

Prayer starter:

Lord Jesus, whatever happens in my life today, help me above all else to follow you. If you give me an opportunity to speak for you, please help me to take it. Give me the words to say.

Day 14
SERVE HIM AS LORD - 2
Matthew 5:13-16

Work in the kitchen ground to a halt when the salt went on strike. The argument was that the best possible place to be salt was surely together, protected in the salt tub from damp and contamination. How shocking of the cook to declare that the food needed salting! How outrageous to suggest that salt isn't really salt unless it's doing what it was made to do! The cook was saddened but determined. If this salt wouldn't co-operate, new salt would have to be found to complete the task.

Secure behind our battlements, the church gets on with insider activities, remote from an indifferent world. The fortress church knows it should do some evangelism, so every few years the drawbridge is let down and a hired army charges out to win recruits. After the mission, the drawbridge is swung back up... Normal isolation is resumed as soon as possible.

If this rings any bells as far as your church is concerned, is there anything you could do to get things moving?

Reflection:
When the salt of the earth stays in the salt tub, when the light of the world hides itself away, how do you think Jesus feels about his church?

It's not 'stay' but 'go' said Jesus: 'Go, then, to all peoples everywhere...' (Matthew 28:19)

Cross purposes

If we really want Jesus to be Lord, we need to tune in to a new way of living.

Blessed are the rich, for they can buy what they want.

> *Blessed are the poor in spirit, for theirs is the kingdom of heaven.*

Blessed are those who are having a good time, for they can forget tomorrow.

> *Blessed are those who mourn, for they shall be comforted.*

Blessed are the powerful, for they will rule the earth.

> *Blessed are the meek, for they will inherit the earth.*

Blessed are those who hunger and thirst for more possessions, for to shop is to be.

> *Blessed are those who hunger and thirst for righteousness, for they will be filled.*

Blessed are those who insist on their rights, for they will get their own way.

> *Blessed are the merciful, for they will be shown mercy.*

Blessed are the assertive, for they will not be trodden underfoot.

> *Blessed are the peacemakers, for they will be called sons of God.*

extra

God wants us to be winners not losers. Our potential with him is mind-blowing! True it's going to cost us; there has to be dedication and hard work. But the rewards make it all worthwhile.

Be a winner

For every winner in sport and society there are many losers. But the modern world has added new ways to lose. In an age of hyper-competitiveness, the price you have to pay to win often seems to be too high. The growing list of failed drug tests among sporting stars in recent years speaks for itself. The long admired 'will to win' has been overtaken by the desperate 'need to win'. The winners have often become losers.

At my school there was a very limited understanding of who could be winners. Those who failed the 11 plus were considered losers. If you were in the 'C-stream', you were a loser. If you left without three A levels, you were a loser. There was only one non-academic way to avoid being a loser: if you were in the first team for rugby. The signal to those of average ability, whether on the sports field or in the exam room, was quite clear: already you are a loser in life.

Today I meet many people who are certain they are losers. By society's standards, by their performance at school or by their experience of family life, they are not part of the elite. The harsh truth seems to be that if only a few can win, the vast majority are condemned to lose. But must it be that way?

NEW KIND OF LOVING

The fact that God knows all about me only seems to make things worse. He sees not only the flaws and limits to my achievements, he also sees my moral failures in full. Surely, if I am without excuse and under his judgment, God too must see me as a loser?

Not so! Have you ever stopped to wonder how much God loves you? You know he loves you enough to have sent Jesus to die for you. But how do you measure such love?

God's love is informed; he's not taken in by the attractiveness of our public image. He chooses to love us in a clear-sighted way, knowing just what we are like. It's a love which reaches out from eternity. It's a love calling out to us from the cross of his beloved Son.

God's love is also personal. Someone once said, 'I love humankind; it's individuals I can't stand!'. God's love is nothing like that. He doesn't just love everyone in a generalised way. He calls us by name, loves us in an intimate way, and comes to make his home in us as our new and loving Father (John 14:23).

We cannot measure the love of God unless we see it's a love measured by the love of the Father for the Son. I don't think anyone else would have dared to claim what Jesus revealed. On anyone else's lips, such a suggestion would have seemed blasphemous. But Jesus is categorical: quite simply, our Father God loves us *as much as* he loves Jesus.

'You have loved them even as you have loved me' (John 17:23).

the
me
problem

It's truly amazing! As much as his own Son, the one without spot or blemish, who has been loved by the Father from all eternity. That's how much God loves *you* and *me*!

What's more, by the Holy Spirit, God pours this boundless love into our hearts (Romans 5:5). The Holy Spirit then delights to testify to our spirit that we really have become the children of God, adopted and beloved (Romans 8:16).

RELEASED FROM THE TREADMILL

We find it hard to take in the immensity of God's love. That's why I sometimes use what I call my 'coffee prayer'. For a few days, every time I have a cup of coffee I pause for a moment and say to God: 'Thank you, Father, that you love me as much as you love Jesus.'

This is the new basis on which God can make us winners. If the only way to be a winner is to be a successful achiever, then for every winner there will be many losers. But you are already loved, already accepted. You have already received the righteousness of Christ, not by what you accomplish, but by what God has accomplished for you. God's unconditional love releases you from the treadmill of human struggle for approval. God decrees you to be a winner in the power of his supernatural love.

Once we begin to grasp this wonderfully liberating truth, we can read with new eyes the passages in the New Testament which use the metaphor of running a race to describe the discipline of Christian living.

The race of life is set before us, and the Scriptures invite us to be single-minded in making our lives count for Jesus. Just as athletes must keep their eyes on the finishing line, not stopping until they have crossed it, we need to keep our eyes fixed on Jesus, avoiding every distraction (Hebrews 12:1-3).

But there's a problem. If you never managed to win a race at school, and if your major contribution to athletics is watching on TV, the picture of life as a race may not be too welcome. As most of us know to our cost, for the favoured few who are winners in this world, there are countless losers. That's why you need to realise that God has entered you in a race that's quite different.

If you will run for Jesus, if you will live for him as Lord, then the old cry of the fairground — everyone's a winner! — becomes gloriously true. Don't do yourself down, nursing a negative self-image. Don't measure your gifts against those who excel, only to persuade yourself that you are a failure once again. For those who run the race of life with Jesus, there are two glorious truths:

- Each believer is loved by God as much as God loves Jesus.
- And, what is more, everyone's a winner!

Day 15
WINNERS NOT LOSERS
1 Peter 1:1, 2

What kind of winners does God intend us to be? In Christ's kingdom, are we guaranteed an easy ride in life? Peter writes to Christians who have been 'scattered', uprooted from home and friends by persecution. What's more, he knows they feel like 'strangers' in the world, outcasts from the values and lifestyle their society considers normal. So how can they possibly see themselves as winners?

It's all a matter of perspective. Others may measure winning in life by what they own or how they feel. But Christians are winners because they possess the gift of a new relationship with God which no one can take away

Think it through:
All three persons in the Trinity take the initiative in making us eternal winners: we are *chosen* by the Father, *saved* through Christ's shed blood, and *transformed* inside by the Spirit. Whatever our outward circumstances, whether life is blissful or tragic, we are winners because God is for us (v 2).

A promise for the week/weak:
'Who shall separate us from the love of Christ? Shall trouble or hardship or persecution or famine or nakedness or danger or sword?... No, in all these things we are more than conquerors through him who loved us.'

(Romans 8:35, 37)

Day 16
GUARANTEED INHERITANCE
1 Peter 1:3-9

Melissa was left a great deal of money when her grandfather died. However, the money was not immediately hers to spend. A generous allowance was available, but the full inheritance was invested until her 21st birthday.

Christians have a similar experience: we live in the light of an inheritance to come. It's guaranteed, not merely by a legally binding will, but by the decree of God himself. When we become Christians, we are already winners beyond the grave. Congratulations, your personal inheritance in Christ is secure! The everlasting riches of the love of God are stored up in heaven for you. A good reason for putting verse 3 into practice right now.

Let's not waste time naming and claiming material things that spoil and perish! In the light of our guaranteed inheritance in Christ, we can claim our present allowance: being shielded by God (v 5), growing strong in the faith whatever life may throw at us (v 7), and receiving an outpouring of supernatural joy (v 8). These things – all gifts from a loving heavenly Father – far outweigh anything the world can offer.

Prayer starter:
Lord Jesus, help me to live today in the light of my guaranteed future with you. Take away my love for... I know there are times when it keeps me from seeking your priorities.

the me problem

Day 17
FAMILY LIKENESS
1 Peter 1:13-25

Victims of conditional love pick up from their parents the impression that they will only be loved if they achieve enough. For some children, that mountain is always too high to climb, and the conditional love stays beyond reach. That leaves many people hurting inside, unsure whether they deserve to be appreciated or loved.

The best of all fathers has adopted us. So how will our Father God help us flourish in the eternal family?

By providing the promises of the Bible and by sending the Spirit of love upon us.

The more we know we are approved by God, justified by faith not works, the more we can break free from the treadmill of a life without generous love and encouragement.

It's a good idea to make a note of any special promises God has given to you, or learn them by heart so that you can bring them to mind when things get tough.

A verse to learn:
'Hope does not disappoint us, because God has poured out his love into our hearts by the Holy Spirit, whom he has given us' (Romans 5:5).

For action:
Since Jesus provides a new kind of loving encouragement, we need to learn to express his life to one another, in our families and churches.

Day 18
IN PERFECT SHAPE
1 Peter 2:1-10

The successful athlete cannot feed every appetite. The appetite for eating junk food or for a lie-in instead of an early-morning run must be resisted at all costs.

In the same way, the effective Christian must decide which appetites to feed. The real problem doesn't arise when destructive desires surface, but when we give them house-room in our lives. Destructive appetites need to be starved (v 1).

The apostle Paul also had something to say to God's 'athletes'. If we are serious about surging ahead, then we'd do well to take his advice (Philippians 3:12-14).

After the initial shock to the system, a routine of exercise can be enjoyable, because we know it's doing us good. Even so, if we want to be in great spiritual shape, we must feed our appetite for God (v 2).

What's more, God's purposes are not fulfilled in our lives if we keep our distance from other believers. We need to see ourselves as living stones, built together as a living temple to the glory of Christ (v 5). Being in great shape means staying close to God personally and getting close to our brothers and sisters in Christ.

Prayer starter:
Lord, I don't want to starve my spiritual health by feeding sinful appetites. Help me get into great shape for your service.

Day 19
SUBMIT AND WIN
1 Peter 2:11-17

Peter was a born fighter. He held strong convictions and was not afraid to stand up for them. When Jesus said he was going to Jerusalem in order to die, Peter tried to prevent him (Mark 8:32). And, when the soldiers arrested Jesus, it was Peter who cut off the ear of the high priest's servant (John 18:10). Both times Jesus' actions and words were a rebuke. If Peter was going to be a winner in Jesus' way, he needed a completely new outlook.

Today's reading shows just how much Jesus had transformed Peter. Now he can talk of silencing those who oppose believers with good works of service, instead of strong words or a drawn sword. The ever-assertive Peter has become Peter the servant.

This is not a cop-out for the weak. On the contrary, it requires greater strength to win through submission than to fight tooth and nail. But this is the new way of winning which Peter learnt from Jesus. Jesus' life, teaching and death all demonstrate a consistent pattern of servanthood. 'For even the Son of Man did not come to be served, but to serve, and to give his life as a ransom for many' (Mark 10:45). Only this wonderful example had the power to overthrow Peter's instinctive reactions.

Prayer starter:

Lord Jesus, help me to be strong enough through your victory to serve others today.

Day 20
SERVANT KING
1 Peter 2:21-25

When Jesus foretold his death, he described it as his 'glorification'. But how can there be any glory in a mock trial, being beaten up by soldiers, and a brutal death? Peter stresses Jesus' perfect restraint as he prepared to die for us. He showed no retaliation, offered no resistance, and made no threats.

In the spiritual realm, the conflict was titanic. When Christ was stripped and nailed to the cross, he stripped the principalities and powers of their pretended authority. When he was raised on the cross by the Romans as a public spectacle, he made a public spectacle of the powers he was crushing.

For men and women Christ chose the way of non-violence and mercy. To satanic forces he is the warrior king, trampling them under foot, as he prepares for their ultimate annihilation.

To consider:

How can Christ be your example today? Where do you need to take the following approaches? –

- a quiet, non-threatening approach to sort out some particular disagreement or problem
- a forgiving attitude
- trampling the devil's influence over you under foot.

Ask for the power of the Holy Spirit to take any action needed.

extra

Givers and takers

If you are going to live as a winner in Jesus, you will thrive on the encouragement of other Christians. And you will help them to thrive if you choose to be a giver of grace to them.

JUST CHECK Look up in a concordance the 'one another' references in the New Testament, to see how important relationships in the body of Christ are meant to be. It's often through the affirmation of other believers that we come to know we really are eternal winners in Christ.

Here are a couple of my favourite verses to inspire your research:

'*Accept one another,* just as Christ accepted you, in order to bring praise to God' (Romans 15:7).

'*Encourage one another daily,* as long as it is called Today, so that none of you may be hardened by sin's deceitfulness' (Hebrews 3:13).

JOT DOWN the names of those you need to be more accepting towards. Pray about ways you could be doing this. Then make a note of those you could be encouraging and start doing this just as soon as you can.

Day 21

LOSERS AND WINNERS

1 Peter 4:1-11

I have just been totally absorbed watching a snooker superstar score a maximum break of 147. It was an incredible demonstration of composure and precision.

But what about winners and losers in the most serious pursuit of all, the game of life?

Ultimate losers often look like winners. They claim to live life to the full, with decadence and dissipation, and sometimes mock those who won't join in. But the judgement of God is inescapable, no matter how confident anyone's claim that self-indulgence is best.

Ultimate winners live now in obedience to God. The simple truth is that if we follow the Servant King, our lives will be marked by service (vs 8-10). Our priority will not be self-gain, but how best to serve others. The SAS may claim that 'He who dares wins', but the Christian motto is more radical: 'He who serves wins.'

Verse to learn:
'If anyone serves, he should do it with the strength God provides, so that in all things God may be praised through Jesus Christ' (1 Peter 4:11).

Prayer starter:
If you know you need to submit to God's control (v 2) over sin in your life, then talk to him about this. Or you may need release from a selfish spirit so you can love others for Jesus.

The right image

In the eyes of Jesus, the right image for those who love and serve him has nothing to do with clothes! It's inner character that counts with Jesus, and it's meant to have a profound effect on those we meet.

T

People notice what Christians say and do more than we sometimes think. We're ambassadors for Jesus *every* day. But all too often non-Christians can dismisss our witness with the words: 'I can't hear what you're saying, because your life is shouting too loud!'

the me problem

Jesus wants his disciples to *be, bring* and *speak* good news. To *be* good news as the kind of people we are. To *bring* good news in what we do, as salt and light in the local community. And to *speak* good news, not only when there is a mission organised, but in letting people know in natural ways, in relaxed conversations, that we are followers of Jesus.

Of course, Jesus didn't meet every expectation other people laid on him. In fact, he often blew their minds! If there was one thing the religious people couldn't stand, it was that Jesus wasn't religious enough! He went to a wedding feast and turned water into wine; he ate meals with very dodgy people; he mixed with crowds in the rough part of town and even spoke with prostitutes in the red light district. Worst of all, he told stories that made people laugh! And so the religious leaders were for ever trying to catch Jesus out, plotting towards his death.

For those Jesus did mix with, the difficult thing about him was quite different. While he wasn't at all religious in an airy-fairy way, he did bring with him a supernatural authority. You never quite knew what he would say. You never quite knew what would happen next. So the crowds were always expressing astonishment at his teaching and actions.

That wasn't all. Not only did he teach with an unparalleled authority, there was a perfect match between his words and his life. When he challenged hostile crowds to name a single sin he had committed, they were left silent. What's more, he showed a supernatural authority faced with those who were sick and demonized. Healing and deliverance could always be expected when Jesus was in town.

NO PRETENDING

I hardly need to tell you that we're not in the same league as Jesus! So how can we demonstrate what he has done for us? The crucial first principle is surely this: no pretending. The Christian faith doesn't need to be packaged like the latest soap powder, in order to be sold to reluctant punters. We are dealing with the revealed truth of God's plan of salvation. How absurd to be false in any way, when Jesus said the truth would set us free.

To be sure, there needs to be a consistency about our Christian witness. There also needs to be a solemn recognition that if our lives are compromised or hypocritical, then we become a stumbling block to those who know us best, actually making it harder for them to escape condemnation and hell.

Our lives will never be perfect. People need to see in us a genuine commitment to a new way of living. But it's unreal to imagine that anyone who knows us well won't see our limitations and the signs of our sinful nature. That's why we can thank God that the New Testament says God has placed his treasure in earthen vessels.

FOR ALL TO SEE

We want people to see that we are genuine believers. But we can never forget that the great witness for the gospel is neither your life nor mine, but the life and resurrection of Jesus. We can't expect our lives to convince others of the saving power of Christ, but we can make sure that our lives won't make it harder for anyone to look to Jesus. We want people at least to sense that there's something more in us than the merely human. We want to be transparent to the presence of the Spirit of God. But then we want people quickly to turn their eyes from us to Jesus, and to discover in his life and teaching God's answers to their deepest needs.

Our witness is more than individual. When we worship together, our worship should have such a quality of the presence of God that the hearts of unbelievers are touched. Our fellowship should be a living demonstration of an alternative society, marked by reconciliation and love. Our praying should have such power, in the name of Christ, that healing and deliverance are signs of Christ in his church today even as they were in the first centuries. Our ministries of compassion and care, counselling and justice should mark us out as communities who live for the benefit of others, and not just for our own gain.

We are seeing in the West a resurgence of interest in spiritual things. New Age books are taking prime space in secular bookshops, as late twentieth century men and women demonstrate a revolt of the human spirit against the narrow materialism of the post-war era. Sadly, at the moment, many seem to be saying, 'Spiritual reality, yes. But surely not in churches!' In a world of broken relationships and fragmented societies, we can be a community of hope. In a world searching for spiritual reality, we are the ones who have found it, for the Spirit of Christ has come to live in us.

We are entering a period when tremendous advances for the gospel are possible, throughout Britain and then on into Europe; an era marked by thrilling church growth and major church-planting initiatives, to establish vibrant Christian fellowships in every local community.

All around us people are looking for something more in life, and we have received in Jesus Christ the very one they need. If we renew our confidence in Jesus Christ, many will like what they see. Let's do all that we can, in this generation, to win Britain, Europe and the world for Jesus Christ!

[redacted]

the
me
problem

Day 22
FULL AND OVERFLOWING
2 Corinthians 1:3-11

Many people think of religion as a kind of spiritual valium, a means of escape from life. But the real question for Christians is not how to evade all troubles in life, but how to react when troubles press in?

Some Christians fall apart, blame God and others, or they soldier on denying there's any difficulty. But there's a better way.

Because we are adopted in Christ, God has become for us the 'God of all comfort'. He is not against us, standing over us in disapproval to see whether we will fail in the face of life's difficulties. God wants to comfort and help us. What's more, the Holy Spirit can pour out so much comfort upon us that there's an overflow, plenty for the comfort of others. And that's the image we should be giving to those who need encouragement: that we care and are willing to share their problems, pain and unhappiness.

It may mean:

- calling on our own experiences (v4)
- getting alongside those in need (vs 5-7)
- spending time in prayer (v 11)
- receiving a blessing from God (v 11)

Prayer topic:

Pray for someone you know who needs the comfort of Christ today. Then let him/her know of your prayers and your concern.

Day 23
VICTORS ON PARADE
2 Corinthians 2:14-17

As the Roman Empire expanded through conquest, battles were followed by magnificent military processions. The triumphant general would march through the centre of a city, followed by his soldiers and the captives they had seized. Crowds would gather to cheer them on their way, while sweet spices were burnt, filling the air with the fragrance of victory.

Day by day, we are part of Jesus' procession of triumph, for victory has already been won through his death and resurrection. When you travel to work or hop on a bus to the shops, you are marching in victory. Whether you are involved in a mission, serving in your local church, joining in a 'March for Jesus' or even establishing a new congregation, you are marching in victory. Your confidence in life is determined, not by your personal success, but by the most decisive event in human history: the resurrection of Christ which can never be undone.

Keep marching!

Prayer starter:

Father God, even though I am sometimes mocked for following you, thank you that I can be certain not only of your comfort and presence with me but of Jesus' triumphant resurrection. Help me to remember today that I am marching in the victory of Christ.

Day 24

KEEP CHANGING!

2 Corinthians 3:1-18

We live in a world of constant change. Our homes are filled with appliances undreamt of fifty years ago. Many people change their car every three years and their house every five. Such is the rate of development that by the time many products are available in the shops the next generation of technology is already on the design table.

Sir John Harvey-Jones, a manufacturing troubleshooter, has repeatedly warned business leaders that the only lifelong habit they can afford is a commitment to continuous change.

Change can be exhilarating, but it's often threatening too, and so people seek refuge in a part of life which is stable and secure. Some churches become a refuge from change – as it was in the beginning, is now and shall be for ever! They close their minds to what is going on around them (vs 14, 15) and drift along ineffectively.

But the Christian response to change is based upon two truths: our God never changes; yet he is totally committed to continuous change among his people.

Prayer starter:

Thank you, Jesus, that in a world of constant change, you and the gospel never change.

Thank you, Holy Spirit, that you are always working to change us, to make us more like Jesus and effective witnesses in today's world.

Day 25

INSIDE THE PACKAGE

2 Corinthians 4:1-15

Marketing and advertising have come of age in the late twentieth century. Successful products can't simply work well, they must also look good.

So how should we 'package' the Good News?

Paul identifies some key principles: everything is done with integrity; we avoid anything devious or underhand. Everything is centred on Jesus: even when exciting things happen in our churches we take care to speak of the glory of Christ, banishing pride. We don't pretend we can save, convert or heal anyone. Rather we declare the glorious and supernatural power of the living Christ.

Packaging is now such an art that the contents can be a disappointment. The relationship between Christians and the gospel is the reverse. God has set the treasure of the gospel in very ordinary and flawed lives (v 7). This wonderfully demonstrates that *no one* earns salvation: it's an undeserved gift from God. And it's often given to the most unlikely people in the world's eyes.

Think of the Christians you know and sort them out in your mind into 'likely' and 'unlikely' categories. Then remind yourself that God's grace is not limited – it's for *all.*

Prayer starter:

Lord Jesus, help me to reveal the presence of your glory to those who know me well enough to see my faults.

Day 26
FREE GIVING
2 Corinthians 8:1-15

the me problem

People in the West have never had so much money to spend, nor so many things to spend it on. Today I invite you to be an investor in the salvation of the world!

- Giving should begin, not simply with crisis needs, but with overflowing joy (v 2).
- Giving should be eager not begrudging; sacrificial rather than stingy; hilarious rather than reluctant (vs 3, 4, 12; 2 Corinthians 9:7).
- The Macedonian Christians didn't just hand over some loose change, they first 'gave themselves to the Lord' (v 5). This is dangerous! When you give yourself to God, recognising that all you own is on trust from him, he may ask you to release more than you intended...
- Paul's says, first be willing, then get organised (v 11). Good intentions are not enough nor spur of the moment generosity. We must act now *and* next week *and* the week after.

Today, many Christians use covenant giving and standing orders, to ensure their giving is planned and delivered efficiently. You may feel you haven't enough to give in this way. But this doesn't have to stop you giving on a regular basis, whatever the amount.

Suggestion:
You can tell someone's priorities in life by how they use their money. What could be learnt about you?

Day 27
BARRIERS BROKEN
Colossians 3:5-11

Throughout history, people have been divided by three mighty barriers. The racial barrier, when peoples assume arrogant or hostile attitudes; The economic barrier, when the poor are exploited. And the sexual barrier, when men treat women as second-class citizens.

The cross of Christ tears down these dividing walls. People of all backgrounds can be united in Christ, breaking free from deep and ancient divisions of prejudice and stereotype.

Because Christ's crucifixion smashes the barriers of human society, we are called not only to speak, but also to *be* and *demonstrate* good news. In a world of lonely, rejected and hurting people, Christ invites churches to be communities of reconciliation. But we must examine ourselves thoroughly to root out racial and class prejudice, and sexual stereotyping.

Prayer starter:
Lord Jesus, burn off our prejudices, take away our fears, tear down the barriers, so that your people might demonstrate the reconciling power of your cross.

Verse to learn:
'There is neither Jew nor Greek, slave nor free, male nor female, for you are all one in Christ Jesus' (Galatians 3:28).

Day 28
CHOOSE TO CHANGE
Colossians 3:12-17

While God's desire and purpose is to renew us in the likeness of Christ, the Spirit will not have room to work unless we co-operate. Paul refers several times in his letters to the need for a Christian to take off the 'clothes' of the old nature and put on the qualities and behaviour of our new life. We need to become *outwardly* what we already are within, by faith in Christ.

There is a double discipline in outward behaviour. First, it's easy to slip back into old habits. They die hard. So we need consciously and deliberately to take off and discard such attitudes when they reappear. At the same time, behaviour in line with Christ may come less readily. The fit may not feel quite right. Don't give up; keep on choosing the way of Christ until the 'clothing' of your resurrection life becomes a part of daily living.

Take another look at the 'clothes rack' (vs 12-14) and pick out the items you are missing. Ask God to give you a fitting!

Prayer starter:
Lord Jesus, if I am to reveal good news in the way I live, I need to know more of your life within. Bring home how much you have forgiven me, so that I might want to forgive others.

Dreams into action

In our church we once spent several months inviting everyone to share their dreams for the fellowship through discussion in home groups. We really want to hear the purposes of God, not only through the leadership but through every member.

ALL AGES On the day of Pentecost, Peter explained that the coming of the Holy Spirit brought the fulfilment of Joel's prophecy. Young and old, women and men, all could now be spoken to through dreams and prophecy to reveal the purposes of God (Acts 2:17-21).

MAKE IT COUNT How about writing down your dreams for your life as a believer? How will you make your life count for Jesus before the year 2000?

Maybe you could begin to make a note of some dreams for your local church. What's to stop godly dreams paving the way to renewal and revival, if we have the faith to turn dreams into action?

THANK GOD that he speaks in all different ways to make himself known to us. Pray about the dreams you have for your life as a Christian over the next year.

extra

WHAT NEXT!

You've finished this book. What are you going to do about Bible reading now? Well, for a start, there are four other *Growing with Jesus* books. If you have already worked through all of those, Scripture Union offers a choice of three different styles of notes for adults. One of them should suit you!

You may order GWJ books and Scripture Union notes from
- your local Christian bookshop
- your Scripture Union church representative
- by post from Scripture Union Mail order.

SU ADULT BIBLE READING NOTES

DAILY BREAD Practical help from the Bible for everyday Christian living. £1.60 quarterly

ALIVE TO GOD Bible exploration for living by the Spirit. £1.60 quarterly

DAILY NOTES An in-depth reflection for more experienced Bible readers. £1.60 quarterly

GROWING WITH JESUS SERIES

the ME problem by Rob Warner

the LOVE story by Lynn Green

the POWER dimension by Michael Cole

the GOD slot by Philip Mohabir

the PRAYER principle by Jim Graham

ORDER FORM

To: Scripture Union Mail Order, 9-11 Clothier Road, Bristol BS4 5RL
Tel: (0272) 719709 24 hr order line Fax: (0272) 711472

GWJ Books	Total
Me problem (£2.25*)	
Love Story (£2.25*)	
Power dimension (£2.25*)	
God slot (£2.25*)	
Prayer principle (£2.25*)	

	Quantity	Price
Daily Bread (£9.20*)		
Daily Notes (£9.20*)		
Alive to God (£9.20*)		
Total		

*Including UK postage and packing. (*Payment with order please*)

Please send me one year's supply of the above notes starting

☐ **January** ☐ **April** ☐ **July** ☐ **October** (*please tick one*)

Overseas rates Europe +£1.50 per subscription. Outside Europe +£3.00 per subscription.

PLEASE USE BLOCK CAPITALS

Name ______________________________

Address ______________________________

______________________________ Postcode ____________

I enclose CHEQUE/POSTAL ORDER amount £ ____________

Please debit my ACCESS/BARCLAYCARD amount £ ____________

☐☐☐☐☐☐☐☐☐☐☐☐☐☐☐☐ Expiry date ☐☐☐☐

In **Australia**, write for subscription details to: Scripture Union, 241 Flinders Lane, Melbourne, Vic 3000.
In **USA**, write for subscription details to: Scripture Union, 7000 Ludlow Street, Upper Darby, PA 19082.
In **Canada**, write for subscription details to: Scripture Union, 1885 Clements Road, Unit 226, Pickering, Ontario, L1W 3V4. In **South Africa**, write for subscription details to: Scripture Union, Millard House, 83 Camp Ground Road, Rondebosch 7700.

GWJ94